"You don't have to be mental here, but it helps"

Alexandria Jones

Presentation by *BookLeaf Publishing*

Web: www.bookleafpub.com

E-mail: info@bookleafpub.com

ISBN: 9789357697095

First edition 2022

DEDICATION

To my Mum, who taught me about poetry and unconditional love.

To my Nan, who inspired me to help others but also myself.

And to my Gran, who always reminds me that you never know what's around the corner.

ACKNOWLEDGEMENT

You know who you are - thank you for encouraging me to be my honest self.

PREFACE

I'm compiling this collection as part of the BookLeaf
Publishing #TheWriteAngle writing challenge
because writing has always been cathartic, and it
inspired me to express myself again.

This is the matter.

During an argument, he asks:
"What's the matter with you?"

Well, my love, let me explain:
I fail at everything, again and again.

I hate myself and how I overreact.
I've made myself disgusting and fat.

In my mind, I'm digging my grave;
Want to scream back at you but I'm not that brave.

Why do I push everyone away?
I know eventually nobody will stay.

And every day is torture.

Update you didn't ask for

Why can't I remember
Your smiles and the softness of your skin?
Or summer days out and winter nights in?
The merry-go-round, warm cookies with chocolate bits?
Why don't I see your face when nostalgia hits?

Why do I only remember
The tears and the fears and resentment?
The rejection and the embarrassment?
Being forgotten and left on the shelf?
Why do I have no sense of self?

My mind has etched a detailed map
On a scrunched up little piece of scrap
Of the open wounds and scars since healed
While I figured out how to use my shield.
Directions are hazy to the happy place,
But I still wear your smile on my face.
The right job came along, and the right one.
Happy memories will be the reward
Of a battle well won.

I'm yours but not in any meaningful way.
I spoke to my brother the other day,
First time in months but it's better than you did.
Why do I always end up feeling so stupid?
Well, not any more.

Hope story

Always careless, I look around
But you were gone without a sound
Like the future abruptly evaporated
And every limb suddenly felt weighted
Not necessarily dark, but now very cloudy
My head was shouting at me loudly
That I failed and I am nothing of value
Strange that it shouts in the voice of you.
Not me.
I think it was taken, not simply misplaced
Spark by spark, eventually erased
I could see no exit, no way to get better
Thoughts crept in, "it'll be this way forever"
Oh it's surviving but not really living
When the eternal night is so unforgiving

Then I found a light in the form of a soul
Returning puzzle pieces to make a whole
Taping back broken bits til they meld
Until I remembered what it's like to be held
By his arms but also in ways of the heart
Colour seeped in to this work of art
I got to a place with light all around it
This is the story of how I lost my hope
But I finally found it.

I should, Because

I should learn to wear shoes in the house
Because treading on your eggshells
is hurting my feet.

I should learn to follow instructions
Because being stuck in your cell
is better than beat.

I should learn not to fight for myself
Because the war is more bloody
And I don't survive.

I should learn to think more like you
Because being an understudy
Is somewhat a life.

I should learn to try to fit your mould
Because the song I sing
Is off-key to you.

I could easily learn to fit your mould
But the thing about it is
I don't want to.

And I cried.

I gave away my life vest so I can't save myself.
I slowly grew weaker as I nursed him back to health.
I watched him play with other toys while I sat on the shelf.
And I cried.

A dark hole swallowed me and shattered my heart.
I knew he wasn't the right one for me from the start.
I painted over our cracks like a work of art.
And I cried.

The sun started shining and the world seemed whole.
The relationship blossomed and brightened my soul.
But the higher the rise, the higher the fall.
And I cried.

If I don't get out now, I'll wither away.
Losing more pieces of me, day by day.
I truly love him, wish I wanted to stay.
But I can't heal here and help him feel ok.
It's me or it's him - there's no other way.
And I will cry.

The Bridge of Life

Life is a bridge
Over waters of trouble
A constant fear of falling in
A constant relief of others
Supporting and helping you
Keep you balance.
Only when they desert you
Can you fall in and drown
Engulfed and overwhelmed by troubles all around
And you discover how harsh
Life can really be.
But there are always those few who play it safe
And walk straight down the middle
That never stumble
Yet miss the ever-changing view along the way.

Fate

Never-ending carousel,
Of existence to end in heaven or hell.

Wonders of your purpose, your meaning
Accompany doubts of the story weaved through your
soul; the power which dictates your life;
Your imagination defines the limit of your control.

Only, escape is futile, a mere false success;
Undefined intentions lead me straight to death,
Though I was destined to do that too.

Time to be honest

A sigh, and my eyes close only briefly.
It's time for me to be honest, completely.
You had your suspicions without any proof.
But now I think I should tell you the truth.

It was raining over us and he was a clear day.
A perfect storm that led me astray.
I didn't know how I felt, but I didn't get far;
The fuel ran out in my getaway car.

It wasn't 'You', it was 'Us', being so unsteady.
You liked the Blame Game and I wasn't ready.
I didn't believe you and I were forever.
I didn't believe things with us would get better.

We were shrouded in darkness but there was a
glimmer of light.
And then we got into another fight.
Wrestling with who was wrong and right.
And I slept alone again that night.
And it's smaller now - that glimmer of light.

Ostriches

Dragging my feet in the same sand
You buried your head.
Why can't I say out loud what needs
To be said?
We're avoiding the elephant striding through the
room.
Who said we shouldn't give up so soon?

I thought you knew but I asked and you didn't
See the problem - should I give you a hint?
Even with conflict and communication issues
I know I should leave but I know I will miss you.

I never wanted to let you go,
But that's selfish, I'm aware.
If you're holding too tight while I'm pulling away,
You'll get burned, and that's not fair.

Now here we are, I've nothing else to hide.
I've shed all the tears I could possibly have cried
In the dark, where you are intentionally living
Ignoring me and the problem, unforgiving.

None was a lie, some of it just pretend
Because the truth brings me to tears.
I love you to the end of the world
But I've been breaking up with you for years.

"Addict"

You use the word "addiction"
I wince and bow my head
Your face full of disappointment
And my heart full of dread

I know the things you're going to say:
You don't know me any more
You expected more of me
What have I done this for?

inhale

I know you won't understand and I sigh.
I'm not a lost cause chasing a high.
But it makes me feel like the girl I was,
When I was happy and healthy and hopeful because
All that was stolen, first by the tears
Then by the agony, and the darkness nears.
Every moment is tainted by exhaustion and pain
I just want to feel like me again.

Sleepy haiku

I wrote you last night.
Words paint our future of dreams.
I wrote us, my love.

Our chance

Did lightning strike twice,
Or did the storm settle just enough
For us to think the embers died out?

Did we fall out of love,
Or were we too young to realise
That's what trust is all about?

Was it a once in a lifetime,
Or was it a once for all time
But we didn't realise what life had planned?

Is it too little too late,
Or is it now our chance
To take our heads out of the sand?

Second-guessing my castle

Building me up, brick by brick,
With compliments and praise.
I guess you never missed a trick
Because I didn't know it was a phase

You made me strong because you believed
In me, or so you said.
Making sure it's you I need,
Cemented in my head.

But the castle we were building,
As the budding queen and king,
Was built on a bed of quicksand,
Slowly sinking to nothing.

The higher the rise, the harder the fall
Or so that's what they say.
Did you build me just to break me down?
Is that the game you play?

In the end, you took a sledgehammer
To my castle, my kingdom, and me
I guess the better someone knows you
The crueler they can be.

Faded in the sun

You are bright as the sun,
Not highlighting my colours
But bleaching me blank.
I grow fainter with the years,
Until I am nothing
With you to thank.
Instead of reaching new heights
Under your rays, your gaze,
I shrank.
Going nowhere with no fuel in the tank.
Every exchange is you pulling rank.
The heat of your words scold me
I'm the toxic one, you told me
My heart sank.

Lost and unsure

Entwined,
But not like two halves of a penny,
More like barbed wire.
Trapped.

Remind me,
How did we get to this point?
Unsure and having to continually
Adapt.

Blind,
To the toxicity glueing us
But I'm starting to see, clear as
Glass.

Find me.
I've been every kind of lost.
Need to navigate back to myself.
Be my compass.

Difficult call

Sitting by the phone, going over what to say
Been a long time coming but it's hard anyway
Admitting that the time we had was just a lesson
Several minutes go past and the silence deafens.

I wanted to tell you this to your face
But the look in your eyes or your embrace
Would completely derail me.
My voice would shake and my confidence would fail
me.

You mean the world to me and that's no lie
I wanted to stay in love and I really did try
But something happened and we switched gears
Sometime over the last few years.

I don't regret our life, our love, our hearts
But it's clear we weren't right from the start
Don't get me wrong love, this is not a tirade
I'm disappointed in how I let myself fade

I wanted to call and tell you the end
But I don't want to lose you, my very best friend
I pick up the phone and think about pressing
Your numbers
But it is too depressing.

The gun.

The battlefield rages
With a fight that's not mine
I followed your map
But you think I stepped out of line.

I'm waving the white flag
But you don't surrender
Your war is unfounded.
And I'm just a pretender.

Words fly like ammo
And you spit them in acid
Burning like fireballs
While I remain placid.

Your opinions, so steadfast
Backed by your mind's army
Weapons in your arsenal
That you use to harm me.

You brought your swords
And I had only a duster,
Defending my memories
With the strength I could muster.

I will always cherish you,
My person, my one.
But you're not the bulletproof vest
You're the gun.

What are we?

"Long lost soulmate"
That's what you said.
Wild butterflies in my stomach
Wild fantasies in my head.

Together too young,
Didn't know what love was,
So we went separate ways.
I regret that because

You saw broken pieces
And didn't think to leave.
You put me back together
Because you truly believed

We are who we are
And we are meant to be
Living a life together
Just you and me.

It's been 10 years now
And you still have the key
To my heart that's been locked
Waiting to be free.

My prince.

True knight in shining armour
You protected my living
When I couldn't see a reason
And the pain was unforgiving.

You came back into my life
And the dragon, you slayed.
The sunshine returned
And eliminated my shade.

You saved me from myself and the beast
And I've loved you ever since.
You don't need a crown to be a princess
You need a prince.

Mum

Showed me light when things seemed black,
I love her to the moon and back.
Forever protecting me from harm.
Once kept me safe, wrapped in her arms.
Her skin so soft and smile so warm
Sheltered me from every storm.
She picked me up whenever I fell
Making it better with her magic spell.
Always teaching me wrong from right
Always with a hug so tight.
Giving it all, without a question.
Leaving room for my own expression.
Nineteen ninety-two began it.
She's the best mum on the planet.

Watching as I bought a home,
Not knowing I felt so alone.
Watching as I built a life
She didn't know the troubles were rife
Too polite to ask, unsure if she shouldn't.
But you came and saved me when she couldn't.

My honesty.

My head is swimming
With secrets and truths
But I'm censoring myself
So there's not any proof
Of the struggles and drama,
The breakdowns and fights.
But this is not the life
I have in my sights.
Then I told him I was writing,
He said it's a scam.
That may be so
But I'm exploring who I am
And to me, that's worth gold.
Although what I write doesn't shine.
It's usually raining and thunder,
But the words are all mine.
Wish I could tell stories
Of laughter and love
But I've written my honesty
And that I'm proud of.